Pitcher Robert "Lefty" Grove

THE STORY OF THE ATHLETICS

Shortstop Bobby Crosby

THE STORY OF THE

# ATHLETICS

JIM WHITING

First baseman Matt Olson

CREATIVE EDUCATION / CREATIVE PAPERBACKS

Published by Creative Education and Creative Paperbacks
P.O. Box 227, Mankato, Minnesota 56002
Creative Education and Creative Paperbacks are imprints of
The Creative Company
www.thecreativecompany.us

Book Design by Wyeth Morgan
Art direction by Blue Design (www.bluedes.com)

Images by Associated Press/Ben Margot, 3, 29, Godofredo A. Vásquez, cover, 31; Dreamstime/Gerald T. Coli, 7 (bottom, right); Getty Images/Bettmann, 10, Don Smith, 7 (top, right), Doug Pensinger, 26–27, Focus On Sport, 6 (top, right), 18, 6 (bottom, right), 10, 16, Herb Scharfman/Sports Imagery, 11, Hulton Archive, cover, Jed Jacobsohn, 2, 4–5, 6 (top, left), 25, 32, Jeff Carlick, 20, Loren Elliott, 30, Michael Zagaris, 9, National Baseball Hall of Fame Library, 1, 7 (bottom, left), 12, New York Times Co., 15, Phil Velasquez/Chicago Tribune, 22–23, The Conlon Collection, 19, Tony Tomsic, 6 (bottom, left); Wikimedia Commons/Boston Public Library/public domain, 7 (top, left))



Library of Congress Cataloging-in-Publication Data
Names: Whiting, Jim, 1943- author
Title: The story of the Athletics / by Jim Whiting.
Description: Mankato, Minnesota : Creative Education and Creative Paperbacks, [2026] | Series: Creative sports: major league baseball | Includes index. | Audience: Ages 8-12 | Audience: Grades 4-6 | Summary: "Discover the Athletics' thrilling journey from early triumphs to modern challenges, featuring legendary players, iconic moments, and the Major League Baseball team's upcoming move to Las Vegas. Written for middle-grade readers. Includes table of contents, sidebars, and index"– Provided by publisher.
Identifiers: LCCN 2025013104 (print) | LCCN 2025013105 (ebook) | ISBN 9798895811030 library binding | ISBN 9798896800569 paperback | ISBN 9798895812297 ebook
Subjects: LCSH: Oakland Athletics (Baseball team)–History–Juvenile literature | Kansas City Athletics (Baseball team)–History–Juvenile literature | Philadelphia Athletics (Baseball team : 1860-1876)–History–Juvenile literature | Baseball players–United States–Juvenile literature | American League of Professional Baseball Clubs–History–Juvenile literature
Classification: LCC GV875.O24 W45 2026 (print) | LCC GV875.O24 (ebook) | DDC 796.35709/79466–dc23/eng/20250519
LC record available at https://lccn.loc.gov/2025013104
LC ebook record available at https://lccn.loc.gov/2025013105

Printed in the United States

Third baseman Eric Chavez

A's
Athletics
20

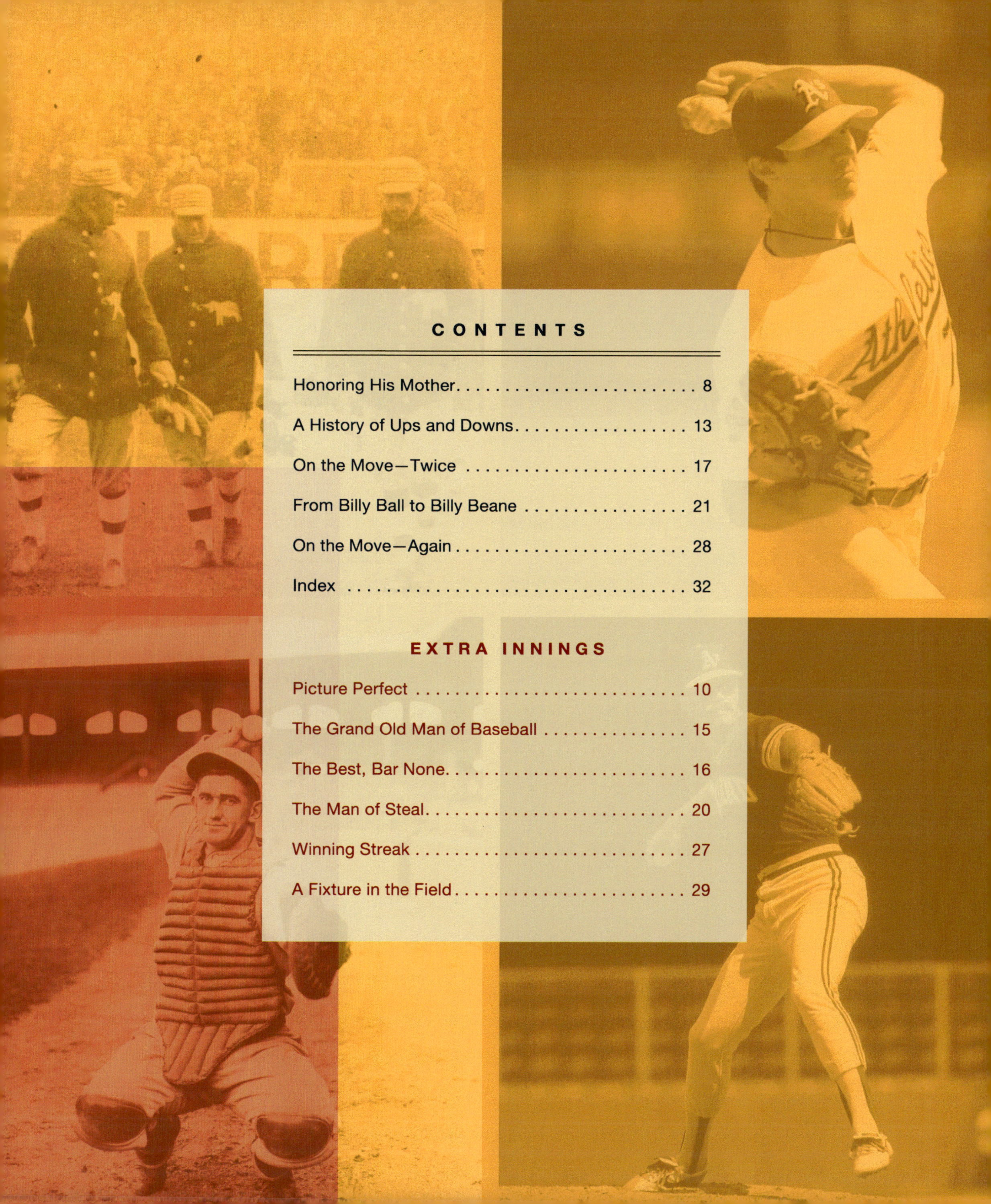

CONTENTS

Honoring His Mother . . . . . 8

A History of Ups and Downs . . . . . 13

On the Move—Twice . . . . . 17

From Billy Ball to Billy Beane . . . . . 21

On the Move—Again . . . . . 28

Index . . . . . 32

EXTRA INNINGS

Picture Perfect . . . . . 10

The Grand Old Man of Baseball . . . . . 15

The Best, Bar None . . . . . 16

The Man of Steal . . . . . 20

Winning Streak . . . . . 27

A Fixture in the Field . . . . . 29

## HONORING HIS MOTHER

Nothing in life came easy for Oakland Athletics pitcher Dallas Braden. He was an only child raised by a single mother who ran a housecleaning service in Stockton, California. In 2011, Stockton was named by Forbes magazine as the most miserable city in the United States. Braden's mother did her best to provide a good life for her son. One time she moved to a different apartment so Braden could play in a better Little League.

Sadly, she died when Braden was in high school. His grandmother raised him in a motel she owned. When he graduated, the Atlanta Braves took him in the 46th round of the 2001 Major League Baseball (MLB) Draft. Braden chose to play college baseball instead. Three years later, the A's took him in the 24th round. It took him nearly three years in the minor leagues to advance to the team, and that happened only because a pitcher was injured. He won his first game, then lost eight in a row.

Braden barely managed to hang on with the team. So when he took the mound on May 9, 2010, against the Tampa Bay Rays—the team with the best record in MLB at that point in the season—it seemed like just another, ordinary start.

For Braden personally, it wasn't. It was Mother's Day, which was always difficult for him in the decade following his mother's death. "I lost my best friend when I lost my mother,"

Pitcher Dallas Braden

**JAMES "CATFISH" HUNTER**

**PITCHER**

**ATHLETICS SEASONS: 1965–74**

**HEIGHT: 6-FOOT-0**

**WEIGHT: 190 POUNDS**

**KEY STATS: 161–113 WIN-LOSS RECORD, 3.13 EARNED RUN AVERAGE, 1520 STRIKEOUTS, 6X ALL-STAR**

## PICTURE PERFECT

"Catfish" Hunter was a rarity. He never played minor league baseball after he signed with the A's in 1964 at the age of 18. Hunter pitched his first MLB game in 1965 and became an All-Star in 1966 and 1967. On May 8 the following year, he pitched the first perfect game in 46 years and ninth in history. He drove in three runs as the Athletics defeated the Minnesota Twins 4–0. Hunter nearly lost the perfect game with two outs in the ninth inning. Pinch hitter Rich Reese fouled off five pitches in a row as he ran the count to three balls, two strikes. Finally, he swung and missed. Hunter's teammates mobbed him. He won the Cy Young Award in 1974 and was named to the Baseball Hall of Fame in 1987.

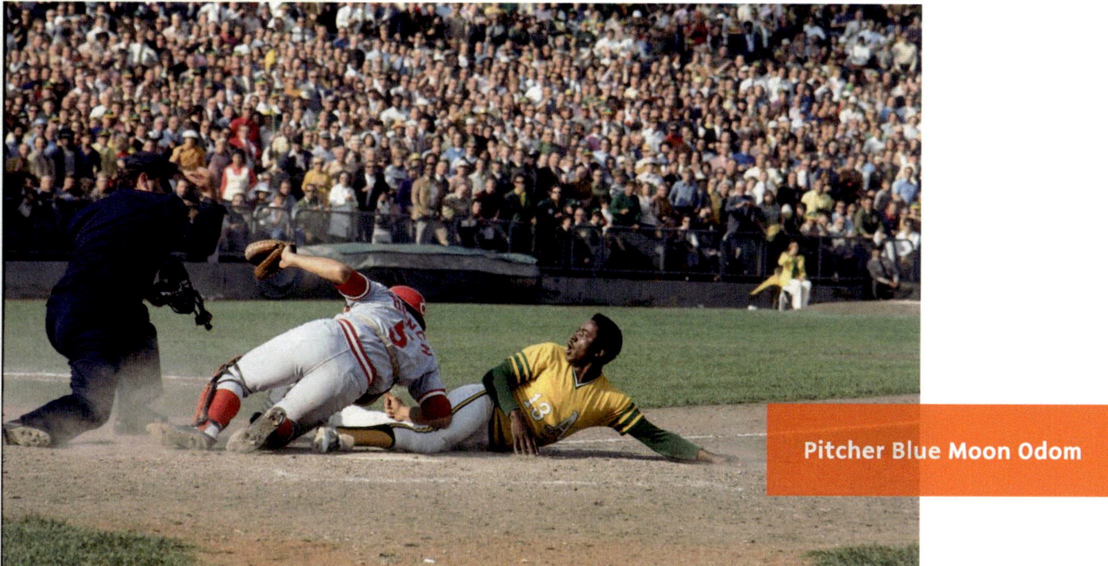

Pitcher Blue Moon Odom

he said. "It's hard when we play [on Mother's Day] to devote the time thinking about her that she deserves."

He overslept that morning. When he got to the ballpark, he didn't have enough time to go through his usual warm-up procedure.

It didn't seem to matter. The young man whose lifetime record to that point was 17 wins, 23 losses and who had never pitched a complete game mowed down the fearsome Rays lineup. Inning after inning, he faced just three batters and retired them. "As I went out there for the ninth [inning], the crowd stood up and cheered, so that's when I knew there was something going on here." "Something" was that Braden was on the verge of one of the rarest feats in MLB: pitching a perfect game. A perfect game means that no batter reaches first base during the entire game. Only 18 pitchers had accomplished that. One was the A's "Catfish" Hunter, who threw a perfect game in 1968.

Braden easily retired the first two Rays hitters in the ninth inning. Then he nearly lost his perfect game. He thought the count on the third batter, outfielder Gabe Kapler, was two balls, two strikes. It was actually three and one. So Braden threw his next pitch just out of the strike zone. Kapler swung anyway and hit a ground ball to A's shortstop Cliff Pennington, who threw to first baseman Daric Barton for the final out.

Braden had just thrown a perfect game! His teammates mobbed him. His grandmother came onto the field and hugged him. "It was so much more emotional than what you would imagine a no-hitter or perfect game to be," said Oakland pitcher Craig Breslow. "Everybody was so happy for him."

## A HISTORY OF UPS AND DOWNS

The Athletics' saga began more than a century before Braden's big day. The American League (AL) was formed in 1901. It had eight teams. One was the Philadelphia Athletics. The name honored an earlier team called the Athletic Base Ball Club of Philadelphia. Former National League (NL) player Connie Mack was manager and part-owner.

Six players hit better than .300 in 1902. They helped bring the "City of Brotherly Love" its first pennant. The team returned to the top again in 1905. It advanced to the World Series. The New York Giants trampled the Athletics. Philadelphia returned to the World Series in 1910. It faced the heavily favored Chicago Cubs. The Cubs rotated through seven pitchers. Philadelphia used only two, Jack Coombs and Chief Bender. The Athletics won the title in five games.

The team won the pennant again the following year. The Athletics met the Giants once more in the World Series. Philadelphia captured its second straight championship. It won its third world title in 1913. The team remained strong in 1914. It was favored to beat the Boston Braves in the "Fall Classic." But the Braves surprised the Athletics and swept the Series.

Third baseman Frank "Home Run" Baker

Philadelphia's dynasty ended after that. The team lost a staggering 109 games in 1915. It fell to last place in the AL. The decline was due in part to the Federal League, which had been founded in 1914. It offered higher-paying contracts and lured many of Mack's best players. The Federal League folded after the season. But Philadelphia continued to struggle. In 1916, the Athletics finished 36–117. It is the worst record in the modern era of MLB, which began in 1901. They remained near the bottom of the AL for the next eight years.

Mack rebuilt the team in the mid-1920s. The new roster included pitcher Robert "Lefty" Grove, catcher Mickey Cochrane, and slugging first baseman Jimmie Foxx.

The 1929 Athletics won 104 games. The team had the league's premier pitching duo with Grove and George Earnshaw. The Athletics defeated the Cubs in the World Series. They locked up another World Series trophy the following year against the St. Louis Cardinals. Philadelphia was the first team to win back-to-back world championships on two different occasions.

The Athletics won a franchise-record 107 games in 1931 and yet another pennant. Outfielder Al Simmons hit .390. Grove won 31 games. He won the league's Most Valuable Player (MVP) award that year. The Athletics faced the Cardinals again in the World Series. Philadelphia had a chance to record baseball's first "three-peat." That means winning three straight championships. The teams split the first six games. St. Louis took an early 4–0 lead in Game 7. The Athletics rallied in the ninth. But they lost, 4–2.

CONNIE MACK
MANAGER/PART OWNER
ATHLETICS SEASONS: 1901–50

## THE GRAND OLD MAN OF BASEBALL

Cornelius McGillicuddy "Connie" Mack was a light-hitting MLB player for 11 years. He hit just five home runs during that time. When he took over the Athletics, he wore a suit and tie in the dugout. Other managers wore their team's uniform. In 1937, Mack was inducted into the Hall of Fame. He retired in 1950 at the age of 87. He won an MLB-record 3,731 games during his career. The runner-up, Tony La Russa, is more than 800 wins behind. Mack's record includes nine AL pennants and five World Series championships. "Connie entered the game when it was a game for roughnecks," said sportswriter Red Smith. "He saw it become respectable, he lived to be a symbol of its integrity, and he enjoyed every minute of it."

**ROLLIE FINGERS**
**PITCHER**
**ATHLETICS SEASONS: 1968–76**
**HEIGHT: 6-FOOT-4**
**WEIGHT: 190 POUNDS**
**KEY STATS: 67–61 WIN-LOSS RECORD, 136 SAVES, 784 STRIKEOUTS, 2.91 EARNED RUN AVERAGE**

## THE BEST, BAR NONE

Rollie Fingers's dad hated his steel working job in Ohio. He packed up the family and drove to California. They couldn't afford hotels. They slept by the road each night. It was worth the effort. The young Fingers became a high school baseball star. Many MLB teams were interested in him. Fingers chose the A's. He began his career as a starting pitcher. In 1971, he moved to the bullpen and eventually became one of the best closers in MLB. He was a four-time All-Star for Oakland and won both the Cy Young and Most Valuable Player awards in the 1981 season after moving to Milwaukee. Fingers is also famous for another reason. In 1972, team owner Charles Finley had a contest among his players for the best facial hair. Fingers grew a handlebar mustache that curled at each tip. He won the contest, and his distinctive mustache made him one of the most recognizable players in MLB.

## ON THE MOVE—TWICE

After its 1931 World Series loss, Philadelphia gradually slid down in the standings. The Great Depression took a toll on team finances. Mack had to sell his top players. The team limped along for more than three decades. In 1950, Mack retired after 50 years as manager. The losing continued. Pitcher Bobby Shantz was a rare bright spot. He won 24 games in 1952 and was named MVP. First baseman Ferris Fain won batting titles in 1951 and 1952.

Businessman Arnold Johnson bought the Athletics in 1954. He moved the team to Kansas City. Nearly 1.4 million fans attended home games at Municipal Stadium that season. But the team finished last or second-to-last in each of the next seven seasons. Attendance dwindled.

Wealthy insurance executive Charles O. Finley bought the team in 1960. "My intentions are to keep the A's permanently in Kansas City and build a winning ballclub," he announced. "Charlie O" liked to shake things up. He named a mule after himself. It became the team mascot. He phased out "Athletics" in favor of "A's." In a 1965 promotion, versatile shortstop Bert Campaneris played an inning at each position. The changes did not help. The team kept losing. Despite his promise, Finley moved the A's to Oakland, California, after the 1967 season.

The change of scenery worked. Future stars such as third baseman Sal Bando and pitcher Rollie Fingers came on board in 1968. Campaneris led Oakland in hits, runs, and triples. The A's finished 82–80. It was their first winning record since 1952.

The next year the AL split into two divisions. The A's joined the West Division. They finished second. Right-field sensation Reggie Jackson hit 47 home runs. In 1971, the A's seized the AL West title. It snapped a string of 39 seasons without being in the playoffs. They had just nine winning seasons

First baseman Gene Tenace (right)

during that time. Only the St. Louis Browns had a longer string of futility. They missed the playoffs 41 straight times between 1903 and 1944. But the Baltimore Orioles swept Oakland in the AL Championship Series (ALCS).

Oakland stormed to the top of the AL West again in 1972. It defeated the Detroit Tigers in the ALCS. The A's made their first World Series appearance in 41 years. The team faced the Cincinnati Reds. The media referred to the series as "Hairs vs. Squares." That season, many A's sported facial hair, earning the nickname the "Mustache Gang." The more traditional Reds were clean-shaven. Catcher Gene Tenace hit four home runs and had nine runs batted in (RBIs) during Oakland's World Series victory. "It's hard to explain how those things happen," he said. "I was kind of in a zone mentally, and every pitch I saw … looked down the middle."

The entire team was in a zone the next season. The A's faced the New York Mets in the World Series. They won in seven games. Oakland coasted back to the World Series again in 1974. It met the Los Angeles Dodgers. The teams split the first two games. Oakland swept the next three games. The A's finally achieved the coveted three-peat!

Second baseman Eddie "Cocky" Collins

RICKEY HENDERSON
LEFT FIELDER
ATHLETICS SEASONS: 1979–84, 1989–93, 1994–95, 1998
HEIGHT: 5-FOOT-10
WEIGHT: 180 POUNDS
KEY STATS: .288 BATTING AVERAGE, 167 HOME RUNS, 648 RBIS, 5X ALL-STAR

## THE MAN OF STEAL

Rickey Henderson did not just break Lou Brock's record of 938 stolen bases. He demolished it. He swiped 867 sacks with Oakland. He added another 539 with eight other teams in his 25-year career for a total of 1,406. That is 468 more than Brock, who is second all-time. In all but one season between 1980 and 1991, he led the AL in stolen bases. He snatched 100 in 1980. Two years later, he stole 130. That trampled Brock's single-season mark of 118. In 1989, Henderson stole five bases in one game. He stole his last base on August 29, 2003. He was 44 years old. Henderson once noted, "If my uniform doesn't get dirty, I haven't done anything in the baseball game."

## FROM BILLY BALL TO BILLY BEANE

Finley refused to pay his top players higher salaries. Many left in free agency. By 1977, the A's tumbled to the bottom of the AL West. Two years later, they won just 54 games. Fiery Billy Martin became manager in 1980. He introduced the team to "Billy Ball." It was an aggressive style of hitting and running. The team rose to second place in the AL West. Left fielder Rickey Henderson stole a remarkable 100 bases, setting a new AL record.

In 1981, Finley sold the team. The A's powered their way to the division title. They met the Yankees in the ALCS. The "Bronx Bombers" swept the young A's. Oakland dropped to a disappointing 68–94 in 1982. Martin was fired. The team had losing records for four more seasons.

The arrival of two players turned things around. Outfielder José Canseco was named Rookie of the Year in 1986. He slammed 33 home runs and notched 117 RBIs. First baseman Mark McGwire earned the same award the following season after clubbing 49 dingers. It was the most ever by a rookie. The duo became known as the "Bash Brothers."

Canseco led the majors with 42 home runs and 124 RBIs in 1988. After one especially long ball, Oakland pitcher Dave Stewart said, "The shortstop could have hopped on that ball and taken a flight to New York." The A's posted a league-best 104 victories. But the Bash Brothers could not defeat the Dodgers in the World Series. Oakland lost in five games.

The A's stormed back to the World Series the following year. Oakland faced the Giants. A major earthquake halted play for 10 days. The A's went on to sweep the series. It was their ninth world championship.

Catcher Derek Norris

The Bash Brothers lifted the team to 103 wins in 1990. But in a major upset, the Reds swept the A's in the World Series. Two years later, even after trading Canseco, Oakland topped the AL West. It fell to the Toronto Blue Jays in the ALCS. The following year, the A's dropped to last place. McGwire struggled with injuries. The team traded him. Without the Bash Brothers, Oakland vanished from the playoff picture.

Billy Beane's arrival as general manager in 1997 would soon change that. He put a system called "Moneyball" into place. The A's had one of the lowest budgets in MLB. They could not compete with the salaries wealthy teams offered. Beane had to strategize to get the most bang for his buck. His Moneyball system relied on advanced statistics such as a high ratio of walks to strikeouts, working deep into the count before putting the ball in play, and defensive skills.

In 2000, smooth-swinging third baseman Eric Chavez and scruffy first baseman Jason Giambi led the A's back to the playoffs. Oakland lost to the Yankees in the American League Division Series (ALDS). "We had a great season," said outfielder Terrence Long. "We played like a championship team ... We'll be back."

Long was right. The A's won more than 100 games in 2001 and 2002. Their 96–66 record in 2003 was good enough for first in the AL West. Pitchers Tim Hudson, Barry Zito, and Mark Mulder became known as the "Big Three." The team returned to the playoffs in each of those seasons. However, it lost the ALDS every time.

**Eric Chavez, Miguel Tejada, and Scott Hatteberg**

TEJADA
4
Athletics
10

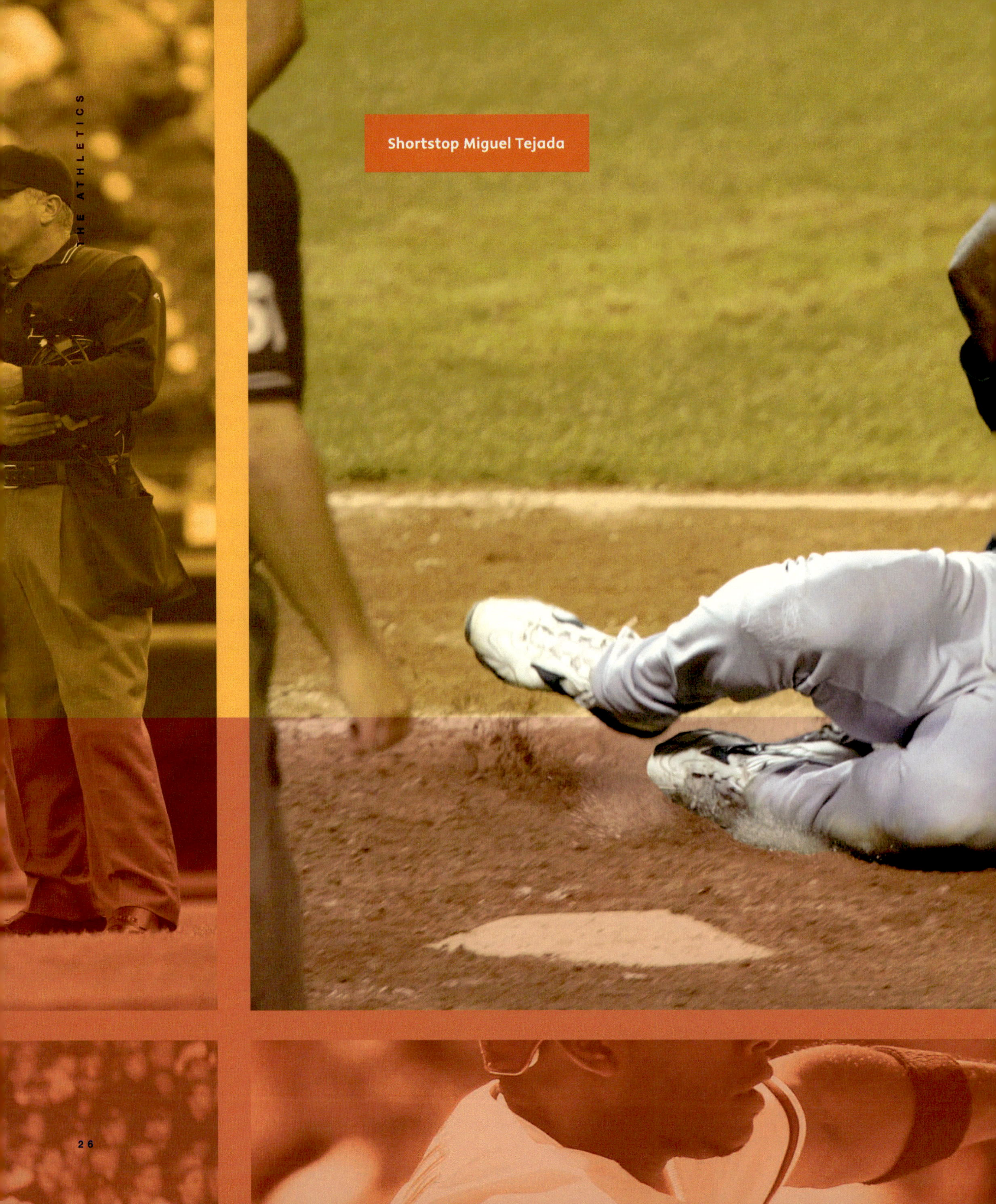

Shortstop Miguel Tejada

## WINNING STREAK

**KANSAS CITY ROYALS AT OAKLAND ATHLETICS**

**SEPTEMBER 2 AND 4, 2002**

Oakland got off to a slow start in 2002. Then the team started winning. And winning. And winning. The A's tied the AL record of 19 wins in a row on September 2 by defeating the Kansas City Royals 7–6 with a walk-off single by shortstop Miguel Tejada. The A's hoped to set a new record two days later. They tallied 11 runs in the first three innings. But the Royals tied the game in the top of the ninth. First baseman Scott Hatteberg came to the plate as a pinch hitter in the bottom of the ninth. The first pitch was a ball. He sent the next pitch into the right-center field stands. Jubilant teammates mobbed him as he leaped onto home plate. The A's had done it! They had won 20 games in a row for a new AL record. The winning streak launched them to a final mark of 103–69. They topped the AL West Division.

## ON THE MOVE—AGAIN

The 2006 A's captured another division title. But the Tigers swept them in the ALCS. Oakland had losing records in four of the next five seasons and missed the playoffs each time.

The team began posting winning seasons again in 2012. Its postseason woes continued, though. Oakland lost the ALDS in 2012 and 2013. It lost the Wild Card game the following season. The A's finished last in the division from 2015 to 2017. One bright spot was left fielder Khris Davis, who joined the team in 2016. He hit more than 40 home runs in each of his first three Oakland seasons.

Oakland seemed destined for yet another losing season in 2018. On June 15, its record was 34–36. Then the A's caught fire. At one point they won 40 of 53 games. They finished 97–65. It was a 22-game improvement over the previous season. But Oakland fell to the Yankees in the Wild Card game. They won 97 games again in 2019. They lost the Wild Card game again to the Tampa Bay Rays.

Oakland finished 36–24 in the 2020 season, which was shortened due to the COVID-19 pandemic. The team beat the White Sox in the first round of an eight-team tournament to determine the AL World Series participant. But it fell to the Houston Astros in the next round.

Oakland continued its winning ways in 2021 with an 86–76 mark. But it finished out of the playoffs. The team lost several key players in 2022 and only managed 60 wins. The A's did even worse in 2023, falling to 50–112.

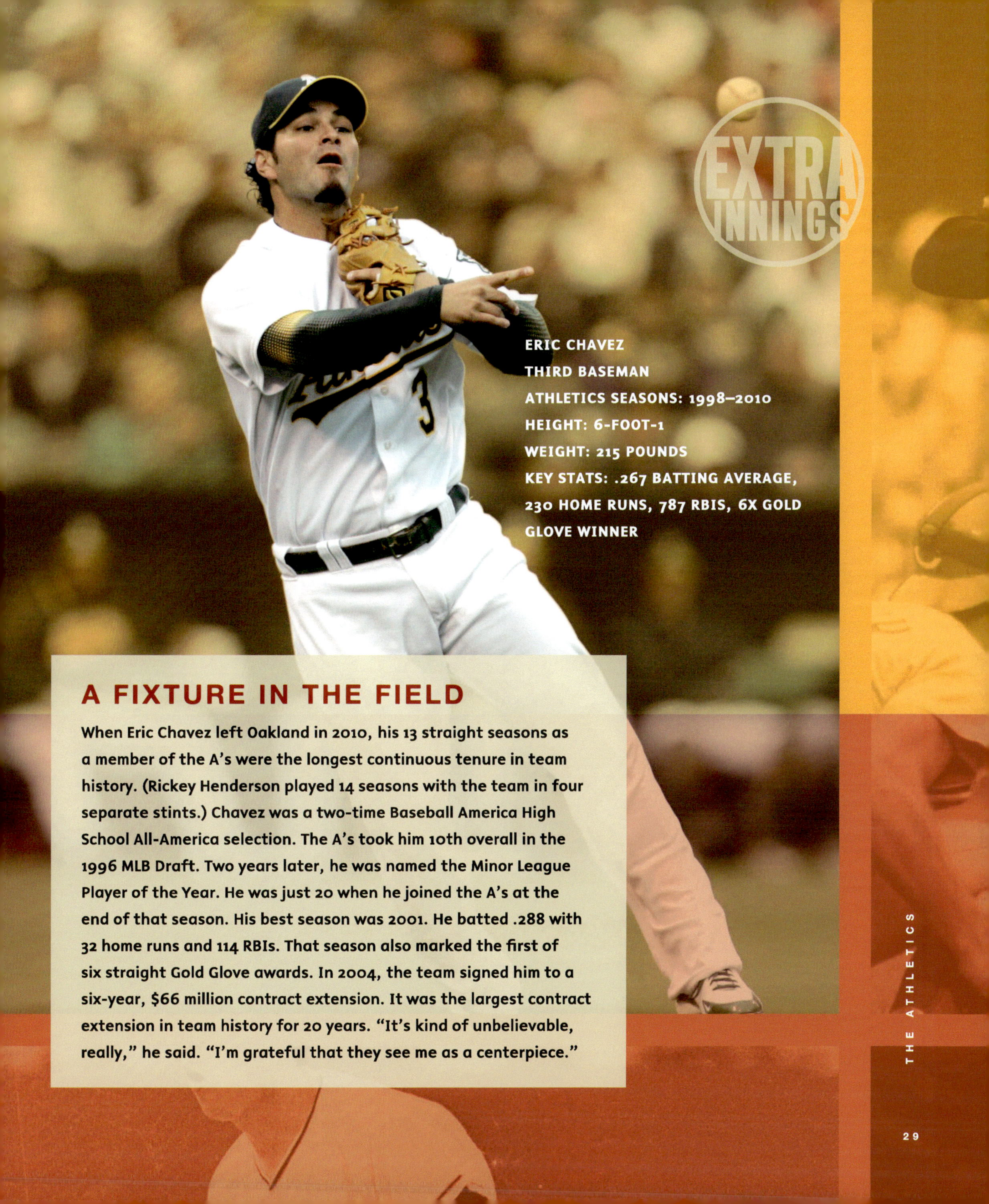

ERIC CHAVEZ
THIRD BASEMAN
ATHLETICS SEASONS: 1998–2010
HEIGHT: 6-FOOT-1
WEIGHT: 215 POUNDS
KEY STATS: .267 BATTING AVERAGE, 230 HOME RUNS, 787 RBIS, 6X GOLD GLOVE WINNER

## A FIXTURE IN THE FIELD

When Eric Chavez left Oakland in 2010, his 13 straight seasons as a member of the A's were the longest continuous tenure in team history. (Rickey Henderson played 14 seasons with the team in four separate stints.) Chavez was a two-time Baseball America High School All-America selection. The A's took him 10th overall in the 1996 MLB Draft. Two years later, he was named the Minor League Player of the Year. He was just 20 when he joined the A's at the end of that season. His best season was 2001. He batted .288 with 32 home runs and 114 RBIs. That season also marked the first of six straight Gold Glove awards. In 2004, the team signed him to a six-year, $66 million contract extension. It was the largest contract extension in team history for 20 years. "It's kind of unbelievable, really," he said. "I'm grateful that they see me as a centerpiece."

Left fielder Brent Rooker

They finished 69–93 in 2024. The team played that season in the knowledge that they would leave Oakland when it was over.

The team had long wanted a new stadium. Their home field of Oakland-Alameda County Stadium dated back to 1966. Las Vegas, Nevada, offered to construct a new domed ballpark if the A's moved there. It would open in 2028. Starting in 2025, the team would play three seasons in Sacramento—more than 500 miles from Las Vegas—and be known simply as the Athletics while the new park was being built.

Starting with Connie Mack's success in Philadelphia, the A's have consistently found a way to reach the top. Only two teams have won more World Series titles than the Athletics: New York (27) and St. Louis (11). Fans hope that the team's newest generation of players will soon bring a World Series championship to its newest location.



Right fielder Lawrence Butler

# INDEX


AL Championship Series (ALCS), 18, 21, 24, 28
AL Division Series (ALDS), 24, 28
All-Stars, 10, 16, 17
Baker, Frank, 13
Bando, Sal, 17
Barton, Daric, 11
Beane, Billy, 21, 24
Bender, Chief, 13
Braden, Dallas, 8, 9, 11, 13
Campaneris, Bert, 17
Canseco, José, 21, 24
Chavez, Eric, 24, 29
Coombs, Jack, 13
COVID-19, 28
Davis, Khris, 28
division title, 21, 28
Earnshaw, George, 14
Fain, Ferris, 17
Fingers, Rollie, 16, 17
Finley, Charles O., 16, 17, 21
Foxx, Jimmie, 14
Giambi, Jason, 24
Grove, Lefty, 1, 14
Hall of Fame, 10, 15
Hatteberg, Scott, 24, 27
Henderson, Rickey, 20, 21, 29
Hudson, Tim, 24
Hunter, Catfish, 10–11
  perfect game, 10, 11, 13
Jackson, Reggie, 17
Johnson, Arnold, 17
Kansas City, 17
  relocation to Oakland, 17
Kapler, Gabe, 11
Long, Terrence, 24
Mack, Connie, 13, 14, 15, 17, 31
major-league records, 8, 14, 15
Martin, Billy, 21
McGwire, Mark, 21, 24
Most Valuable Player (MVP), 14, 17
Mulder, Mark, 24
Municipal Stadium, 17
"Mustache Gang," 18
Pennington, Cliff, 11
Philadelphia, Pennsylvania, 13, 14, 17, 31
  relocation to Kansas City, 17
playoffs, 17, 18, 24, 28
  Wild Card, 28
Rookie of the Year Award, 21
Shantz, Bobby, 17
Simmons, Al, 14
Stewart, Dave, 21
Tenace, Gene, 18
Tejada, Miguel, 24, 27
world championships, 14, 21
World Series, 13, 14, 15, 17, 18, 21, 24, 28, 31
Zito, Barry, 24